MW01596358

I'M A MOVIN' BABY II

Let's keep movin'...

Penny Hines

AuthorHouse™ LLC
1663 Liberty Drive
Bloomington, IN 47403
www.authorhouse.com
Phone: 1-800-839-8640

© 2013 Penny Hines. All Rights Reserved.

No part of this book may be reproduced, stored in a retrieval system,
or transmitted by any means without the written permission of the author.

Published by AuthorHouse 09/10/2013

ISBN: 9781477289426 (sc)
         9781477289433 (eb)

Because of the dynamic nature of the Internet, any web addresses or links contained in this book may have changed
since publication and may no longer be valid. The views expressed in this work are solely those of the author and do
not necessarily reflect the views of the publisher, and the publisher hereby disclaims any responsibility for them.

authorHOUSE®

This book is dedicated to all of the children and parents who have touched my life and inspired me to keep doing what I do. Thank you to my family and friends who have encouraged me and supported me to live my dreams. I feel so blessed to be on this wonderful journey. I wish you a healthy, happy and active life!

I'm a Movin' Baby,
growing up fast.
We make memories,
ones that last.

Lay me down,
gently on my back.
Move my toy
for my eyes to track.

Move my toy
from left to right.
Movin' my eyes
helps my sight.

Move my toy to my knee
and then to my nose.
Put my toy on my belly,
then move it to my toes.

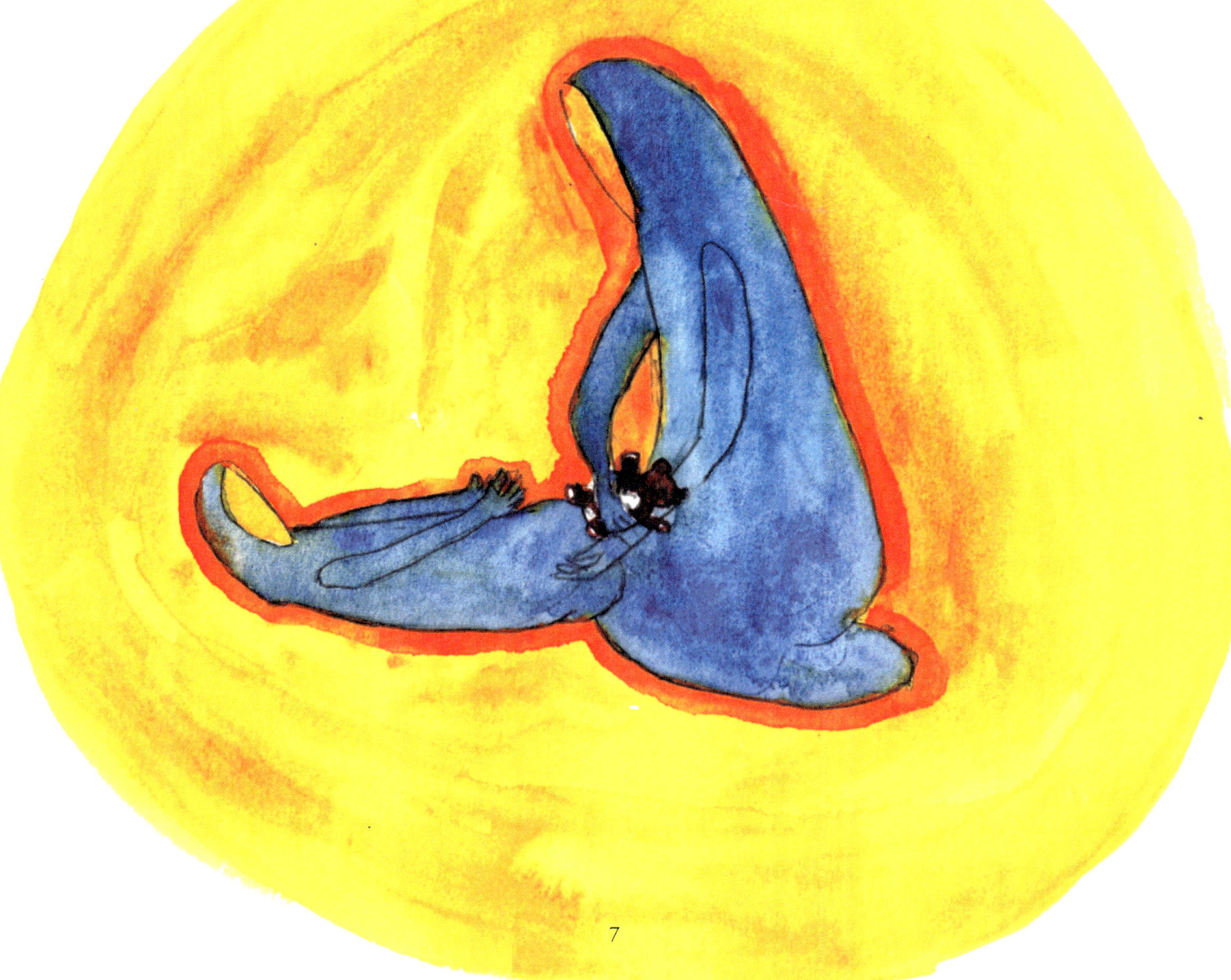

Now bend my legs,
roll me up in a ball.
Then stretch my legs
and make me tall.

Roll me back and forth
from side to side.
Roll me nice and easy
like I'm on a ride.

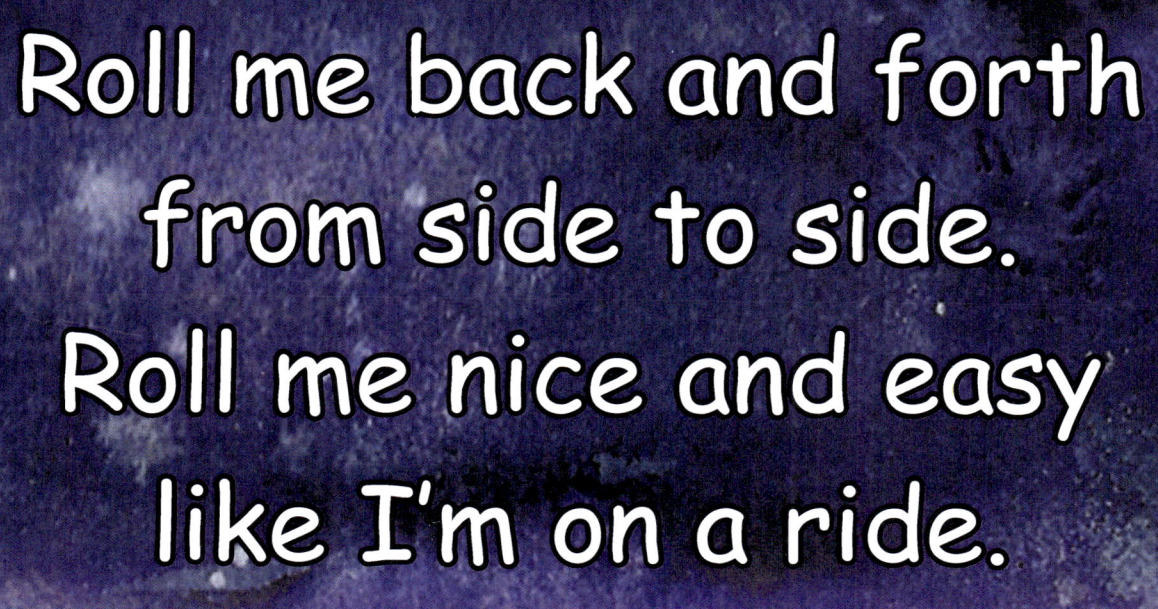

Now sit me up
so I can see.
Hold me at my hips,
so my hands are free.

Lean me to the left
and lean me to the right.
I'll try to stay up
with all my might.

Now cover my eyes,
then touch my toes.
Move my hands to my tummy
and then my nose.

Put my hands on my belly
no time to rest.
Now clap my hands,
I'll do my best.

I'm a Movin' Baby,
growing up fast.
We make memories,
ones that last.

Move my hands
to tap my knee.
Go left then right,
say one two three.

Now tap my shoulder
then tap it more.
Count one and two
and three and four.

Feel so happy
and so alive!
Clap our hands
and count to five.

Now point your finger
and tap my toes.
Count each one
then tap my nose.

Tap hands to feet
say one two three.
Movin' my body,
now look at me!

Roll me to my belly
it's tummy time now.
Movin' to my belly,
we all say WOW!

Pat my hands
and tap the floor.
Tap one, tap two,
tap three and four.

Now tummy time
is a real good way.
Movin' my body
and learning to play.

Keep me on my tummy
I'm not quite done.
Please SMILE at me,
Say three two one.

I'm a Movin' Baby,
growing up fast.
We make memories,
ones that last.

Roll me back to my tummy,
to have more fun!
I need to learn to crawl,
before I run.

Now hold me up
on my hands and knees.
Rock me back and forth,
move like dancing trees.

Now time to crawl,
no time to sleep.
We crawl and creep,
go beep beep beep.

Move me back into sitting
from my hands and knees.
So I can sit up
as big as you please ☺

Now time to wave,
with just one hand.
Then wave them both,
like leading the band.

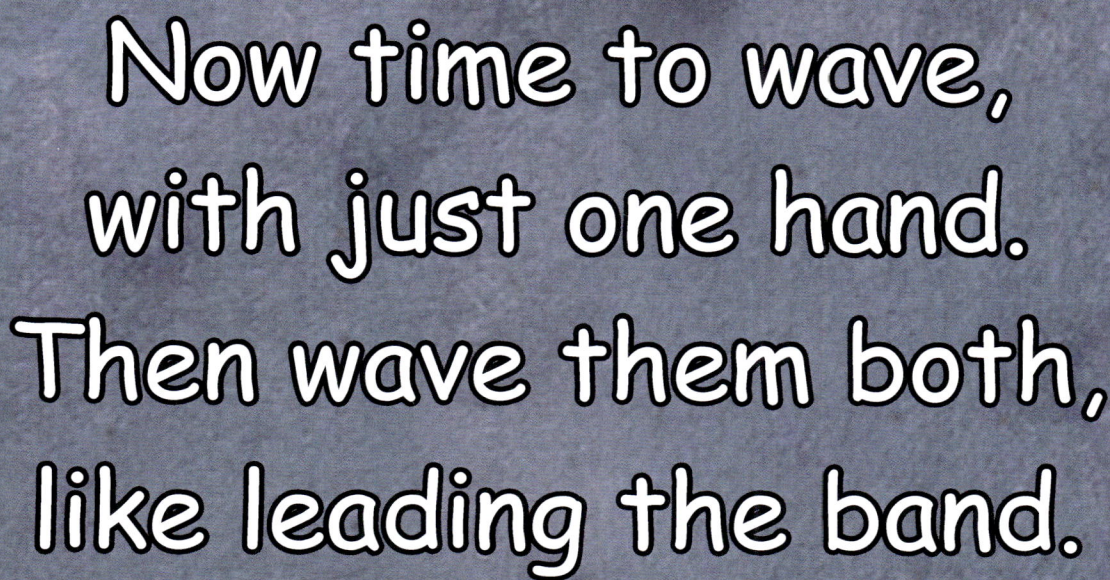

Clap my hands,
say one two three.
Cross my body
and tap my knee.

Move my hands
from hips to toes.
Tap hips and toes,
say row row row.

Movin' our heads,
move them all around.
Now tap my heels,
make a silly sound.

Clap my hands,
say one two three.
Movin' can be fun
when you play with me.

Movin' our body,
move it all about.
Then we make
a great big shout!

I'm a Movin' Baby,
growing up fast.
We make memories,
having a BLAST!

THANK YOU JOANNE LEVI FOR YOUR BEAUTIFUL ART!

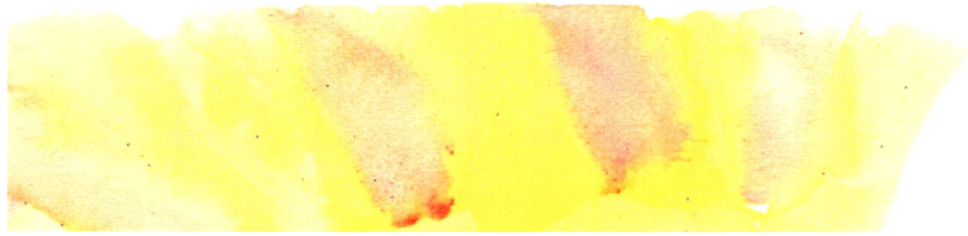

About the Art and the Artist

The art that Joanne created for I'm A Movin' Baby is very special to her because the figure came to her straight out of her dreams! The figure is a guide. How fitting it is to have this guide lead you on a fun journey of connection with your child. When Joanne is not creating art, she is a Licensed Massage Therapist in Centerville, Ohio. You can contact her through her facebook page at Sacred Arts massage therapy/facebook.com. Joanne would like to thank Penny Hines for an amazing experience, Carla for suggesting her art and a special thank you to her partner Guy who has lots of patience!

NUTRITION AND HEALTH COACHING

Penny Hines MS OTR/L, CHC

Occupational Therapist

Certified Health Coach

www.pennyhines.com or info@pennyhines.com

48037940R10024

Made in the USA
Lexington, KY
14 August 2019